Imani's Heart
The Dancing Angel

by Abigail Jefferson
and Chaka Bedell

illustrated by Alvin Burts

PUBLISHED BY

CJW Associates

MARYLAND, U.S.A.

"Imani's Heart"

CJW Associates
PO Box 90728
Washington, DC 20090
www.imani7.com

Book design by Design to Spec, LLC
www.designtospec.com
Edited by Leslie German and Audrey
Carbine
Photography by Cecelia Jackson

Signature Book Printing, Inc.
www.sbpbooks.com
Printed in Hong Kong

Consultants:
Darren Coleman, advisor and author
www.darrencoleman.net
Dr. Audrey Lucas, Psychologist and Parent's
Guide.

LIbrary of Congress-in-Publication Data
Jefferson, Abigail and Bedell, Chaka
Imani's Heart/by Abigail Jefferson and
Chaka Bedell; illustrated by Alvin Burts.
Summary: Imani, a dancing angel's visit to
earth and her impact, lessons on others.

ISBN 0-9724003-2-X

LCCN TXu1-240-675

Imani completed her mission and life.

1. She was born at Washington Adventist Hospital, a
Seventh Day Adventist hospital.
2. She was in the seventh grade.
3. She danced for seven years.
4. She was the seventh member of her immediate family.
5. She passed away on 12/02/02 which equals 7.
6. She was placed in the earth on 12/7/02.
7. She was placed in the earth the seventh day of the
week (Saturday).

Coincidence or Fate?

Every child today is a
gift for our tomorrow.

One day, ten-year-old Chaka came home from school looking very sad. Tears trickled down her cheeks. She slammed the front door, angrily kicked the snow from her boots, raced up the stairs, threw down her bookbag, and plopped onto her bed.

Chaka's mother sat on the edge of the bed and wiped away Chaka's tears. Struggling to hold back her sobs, Chaka spoke in a whisper, "Today my best friend Imani died. I think she's gone to live above the clouds. I hope she's happy there. Mommy, why did Imani have to die? Will I ever see her again?"

"Imani is now an angel and she will always be alive in your heart and in your memories," replied Chaka's mother. She gave Chaka a gentle kiss on the cheek and said, "I have a story. It's called *Imani's Heart, the Dancing Angel."*

Once upon a time, there was a little angel named Imani. She was a dancing angel. She loved leaping, hopping, skipping, jumping, prancing and twirling. When Imani danced, her eyes sparkled liked the stars, and her smile lit up the sky like the sun and the moon. Two thick black fuzzy braids dangled alongside her cinnamon-brown face. Dancing filled Imani's heart with love.

One day, while Imani danced, she stopped to rest on a puffy cloud. The cloud was as white as the fresh snow on the ground. As she relaxed, she looked down and saw planet Earth, and thought, "Ooooh, there are lots of people dancing down there. And tons of good food, too. Sure looks like a fun place to visit." So, Imani went to the sky god, Oludamare, and asked, "Pleeeease, pretty please, may I go to Earth?"

*O*ludamare, frowned and wrinkled his fore-head. He folded his muscular arms, placed his finger on his shiny bald head, and thought deeply. As Oludamare pondered an answer, he slid his hand slowly down his deep, rich-colored chocolaty face, and then gently tugged on the tip of his salt and pepper beard. Soon, a loving smile appeared on Oludamare's face, revealing a full set of pearly white teeth and one diamond-studded gold tooth right in front.

Oludamare cautioned Imani, "Planet Earth was created to be a fun and loving place. Unfortunately, it has not turned out that way. Many people on Earth have broken hearts."

"If you grant me my wish," Imani pledged, "I will fill the heart of every person I meet with love." Oludamare agreed that Imani could go to Earth. He said, "Okay, Imani, you can go, but you must promise me you will always dance, because dancing fills your heart with love." Imani promised.

*I*mani happily picked her Earth parents and eagerly took off for her new home. As soon as she arrived on Earth, Imani's words began to come true. Her family's hearts leaped with joy when they laid eyes on their new baby girl. They were very happy, indeed.

*B*ut as time went by, Imani started to grow and she realized that her family wasn't always happy. Sometimes they were sad and other times they were mad.

Sometimes they were angry with Imani, "Girl, we love you, but you need some time out. Go to your room!" Imani wondered, "How can I keep my promise to Oludamare? I'm supposed to fill people's hearts with love so they can be happy. What can I do?"

After thinking and thinking, Imani came up with an answer, "I need to meet more people, bring them together, and then fill their hearts with love."

*I*mani went throughout her neighborhood meeting lots of new people. People were washing their cars, barbecuing, dancing and listening to music. Some people were laughing and singing. Others were yelling, fussing and fighting. Imani went to her neighborhood school. Some children were smiling, playing ring games, jumping rope and playing hopscotch. They were having fun.

Others were pushing, shoving, bullying and crying. Imani wondered, "Why isn't everyone happy?" She called on Oludamare, "What can I do?" Oludamare whispered into Imani's ear, "Remember to do what makes you happy, Imani. Remember to dance. Remember to dance."

Imani remembered how much she loved dancing in heaven, and she wanted her Earth friends and relatives to feel this love, too. Imani decided to have a big dance recital and she invited many friends, neighbors, and relatives.

On the day of the recital, Imani wore a ruby-red tutu with silver sparkles in her hair and golden slippers on her feet. She performed ballet, hip-hop, tap, African dance, sacred dance and jazz dance. She leaped into the sky, twirled pass the moon, hopped over the stars, skipped around the planets, and finally took a bow. As her friends and relatives watched, their eyes twinkled with delight. Imani could see that their hearts were filled with love as she danced her way back to heaven. Imani, the dancing angel, was happy because she had kept her promise to Oludamare, the sky god. She remembered to do what made her happy. She remembered to dance. And she shared her dance with others, and their hearts were filled with love.

"The End," said Chaka's mommy.

A smile brightened Chaka's face. She gave her mother a great big hug and said, "Whenever I think of Imani, I will remember her dancing and my heart, too, will be filled with love."

Dear Reader,

Your choice to read this story is the beginning of an experience that we hope you'll enjoy, cherish and share with others about a special gift that we have called "a child."

This story was developed from a real-life dream into this beautifully illustrated children's book. It's about our daughter, Imani Wilson, an angel, a writer and dancer, a gift from God. We had her in our lives for twelve wonderful years. Through this experience with our daughter we are devoted to live our lives more fully and generously, especially with youth, because they are valuable and precious symbols of what's ahead for our future.

We also decided that the book needed to be published to help explain the process that we witnessed of life and death. We know and sincerely feel that God is guiding this journey of healing and understanding, and strengthening us daily. We want others to know that it's ok to talk, shout, cry and ask questions. We know that letting go of a child is impossible and our instinct as parents is to refuse to do it. But as survivors we have no choice but to make this experience our own; Imani's spirit is what we have to offer. We have regrets for all the experiences that we will never share with our daughter, but we were blessed with many memories of happiness to celebrate and share with others.

It is our hope that others who are grieving the loss of a loved one can use this book to capture our understanding of how to celebrate life's purpose. In a thank-you letter written to us by Imani and found after her departure, the "good days and bad days" serve as a positive reminder that she knew her life's purpose. It is not in sadness or through a desire for sympathy that we share these experiences, but in acceptance and with deep appreciation and humility.

Although Imani is gone, the bond and time we shared is still very strong with family and friends: in our home, our memories, through her writings and so much more! We hold on to those fond memories because they are precious gifts that provide us with peace and closeness to her. It is always a delight to hear others mention her name and to know that this book is a discovered treasure to all that read it. In our search for understanding, we discovered there is no word to describe us as parents who have lost a child. We discovered over time that our pain, confusion and search for a way to move on is not determined by us, but we are comforted with a spiritual knowledge that with time, all things heal.

Thank you,

Carlene & Jerry Wilson
CJW Associates

P.S. Imani, until we meet again, we know that you have found peace in heaven's hands!

Imani Wilson

1990-2002

Born in Takoma Park, MD, on April 28, 1990 to Jerry & Carlene Wilson, Imani represented strength, courage, character and love. Imani means "faith" in the Swahili language of East Africa. She was named by her sister, Tyanne Wilson. Imani was a seventh-grader at Andrew Jackson Middle School in Prince George's County Public Schools in the Washington, D.C. metropolitan suburban area, and also attended John E. Howard, and Bradbury Heights elementary schools. She loved school and had a strong desire to learn. Imani enjoyed traveling, talking on the telephone, shopping and spending time on the computer while listening to music. She was a great fan of the rappers Lil'Bow Wow and Lil' Romeo and her sister, Camille Wilson.

Imani lived 12 fulfilled years and had a compassionate and humble spirit. She was intelligent, curious, and accomplished all that she desired. Imani had a love for dancing and choreography. Her vision was to open a school of dance for children. For seven years, Imani was a member of the ASA Dance Academy & Company in Washington D.C., where she studied ballet, jazz, modern, tap and spiritual dance. She had a beautiful smile and leaves a legacy of wit and wisdom; Imani's congenital heart defect required her to undergo several surgeries, but due to complications her life ended in December 2002.